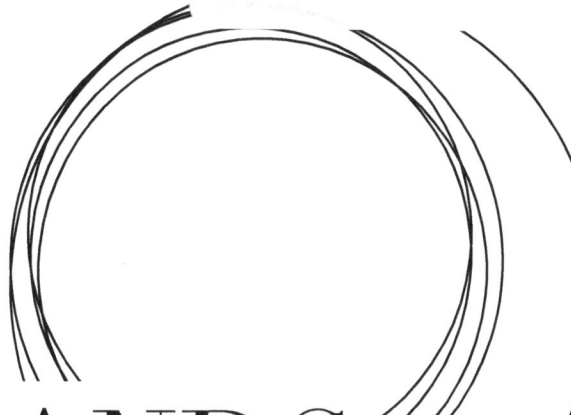

CLAP YOUR HANDS

F I MADE A MASSIVE DRAWING?

NDERSTOOD AND COULD PROCESS MY HUMAN EXPERIENCES? WOULD I DIE?

BREATHE?   OR WOULD I LIVE L

OR WOULD I BE SMARTER?

I DONT KNOW.

Clap Your Hands

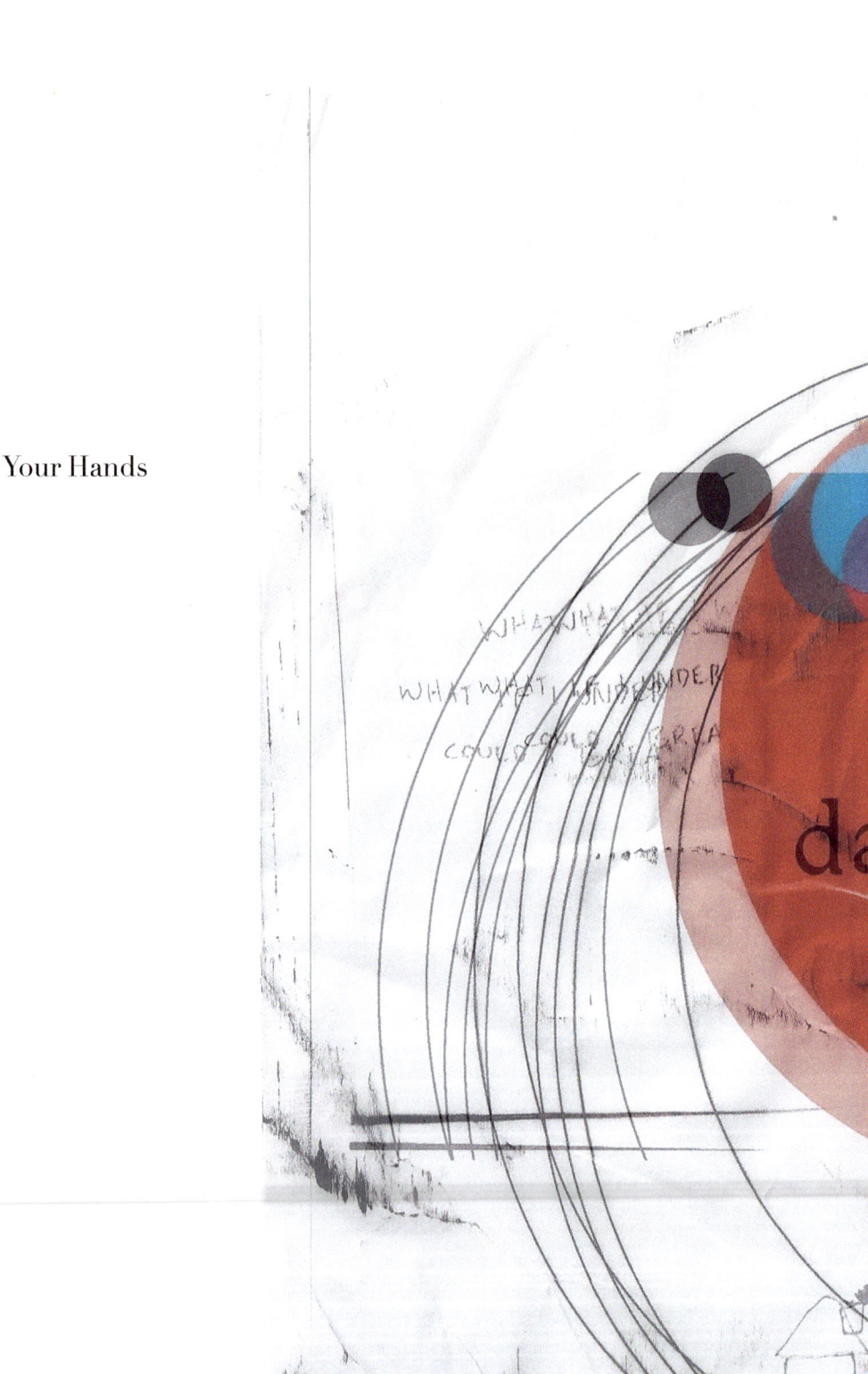

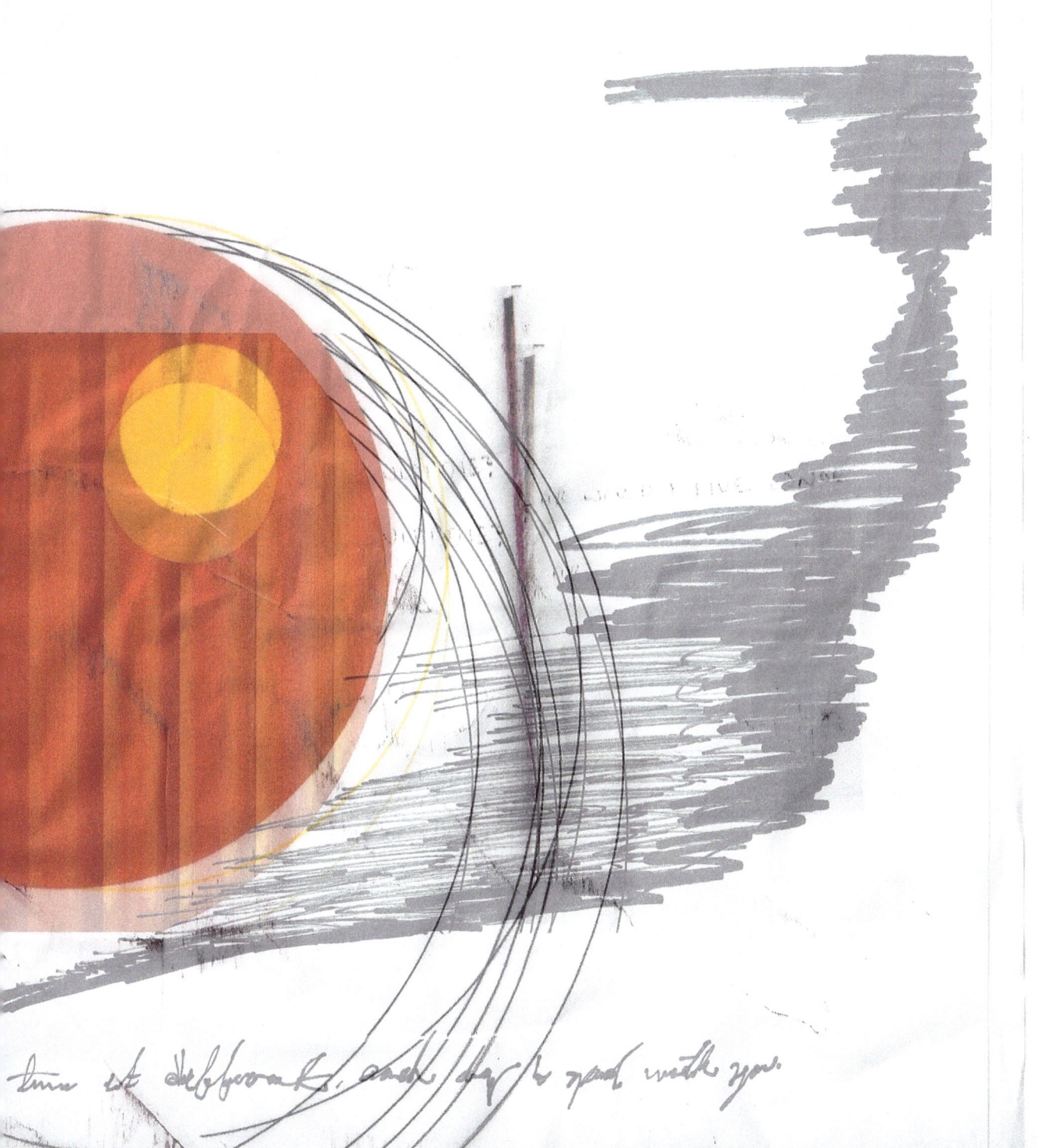

time est differente, each day to speak with you.

Published by
Elaina L. Buie

visit the blog at http://www.elainerbuie.blogspot.com/

© 2010 Elaina L. Buie

Edited by Joshua Son

ISBN 978-0-557-94562-7

9 780557 945627   90000

The art work in this book was created spontaneously while listening to Grizzly Bear's *"On a Neck, on a Spit."*

I highly recommend listening to the song while reading the book.

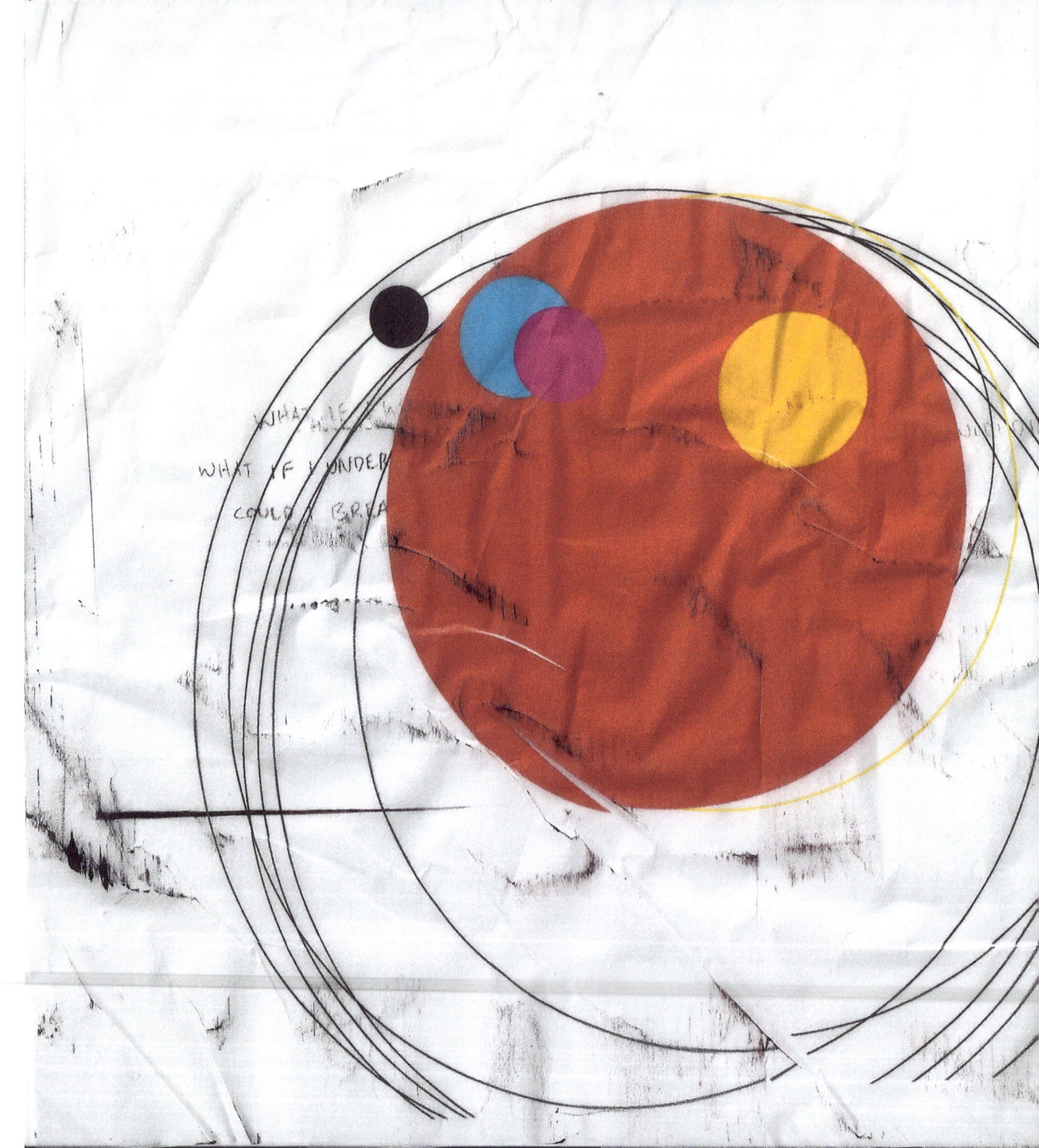

This is a book about love and other things.
But mostly love.

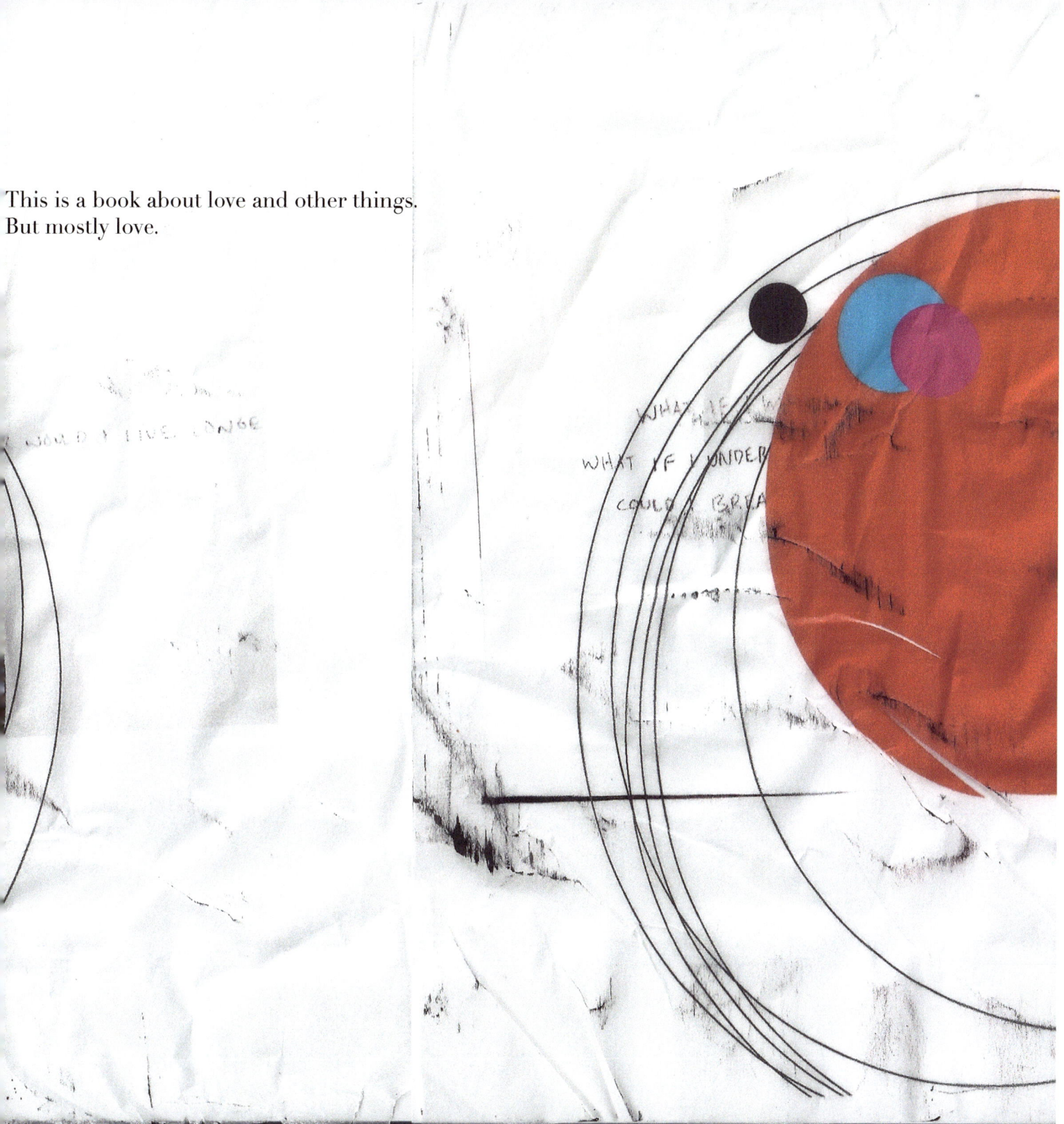

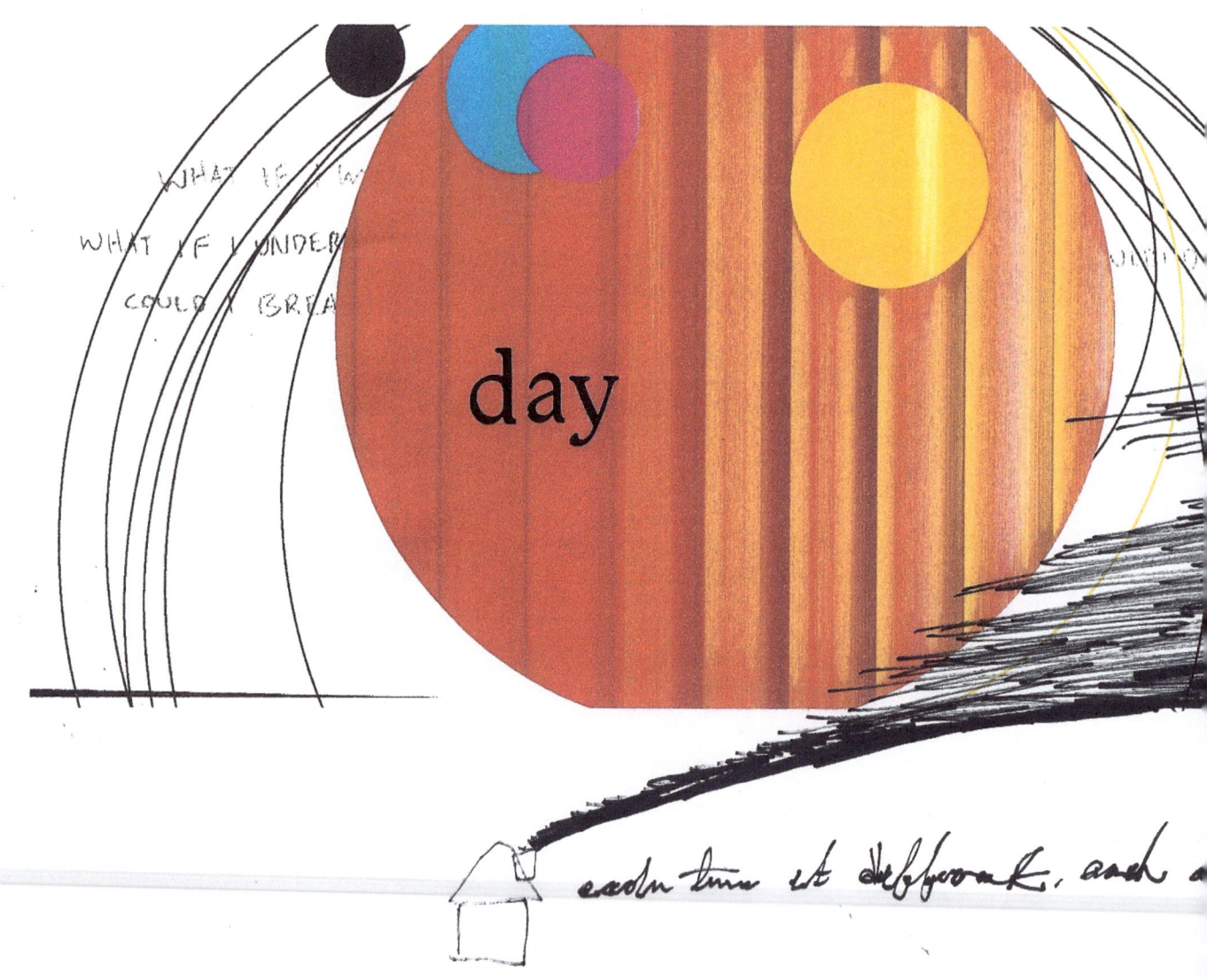

day

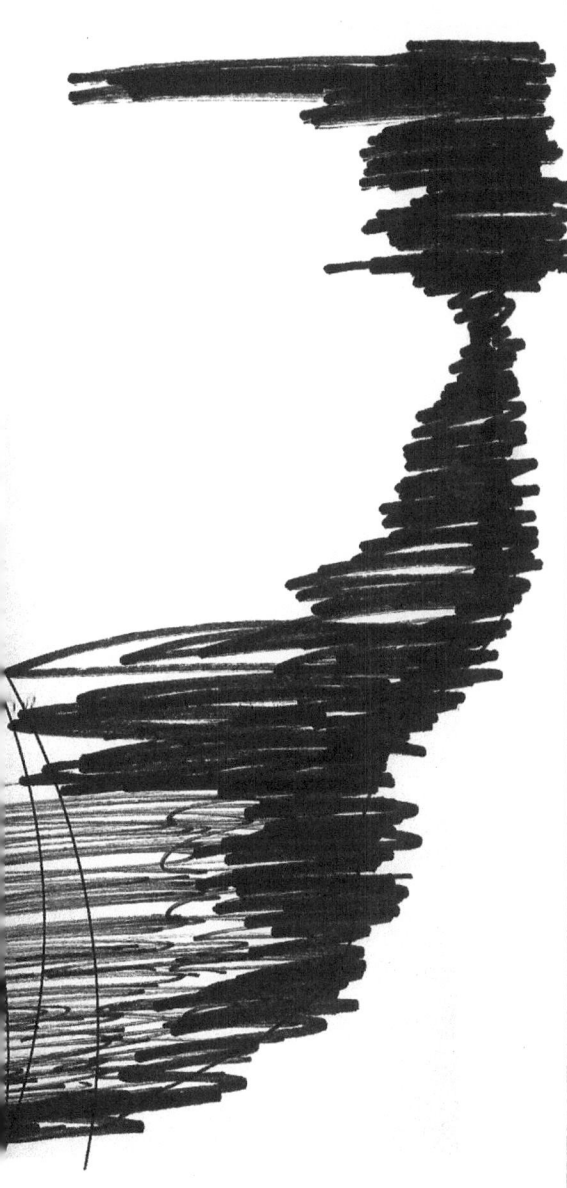

1) If you've ever loved someone who didn't
love you back, clap your hands.

2) If you remember the time we snuck into the stadium
together, clap your hands.

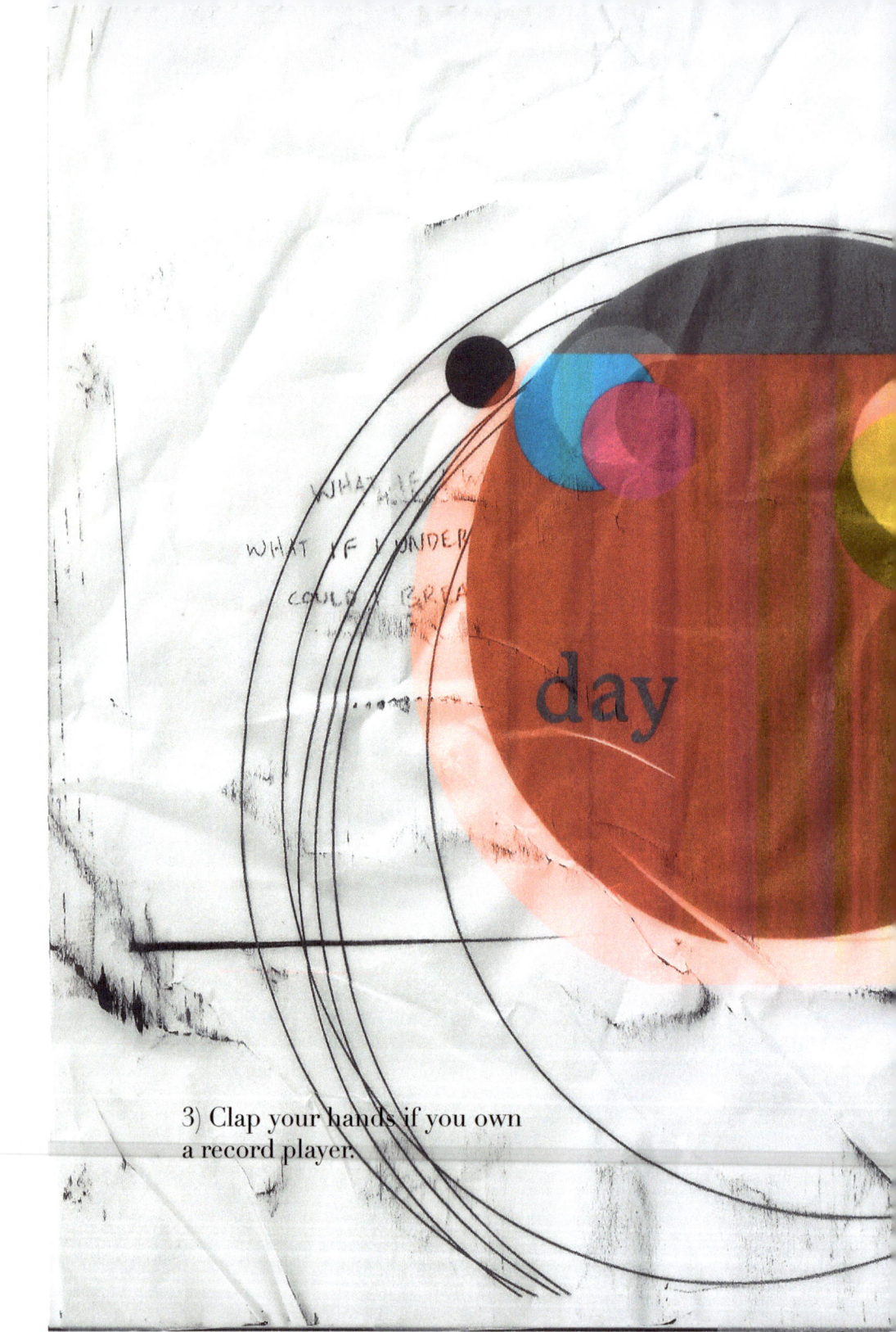

WHAT IF...
WHAT IF I WONDER
COULD I BREA...

day

3) Clap your hands if you own
a record player.

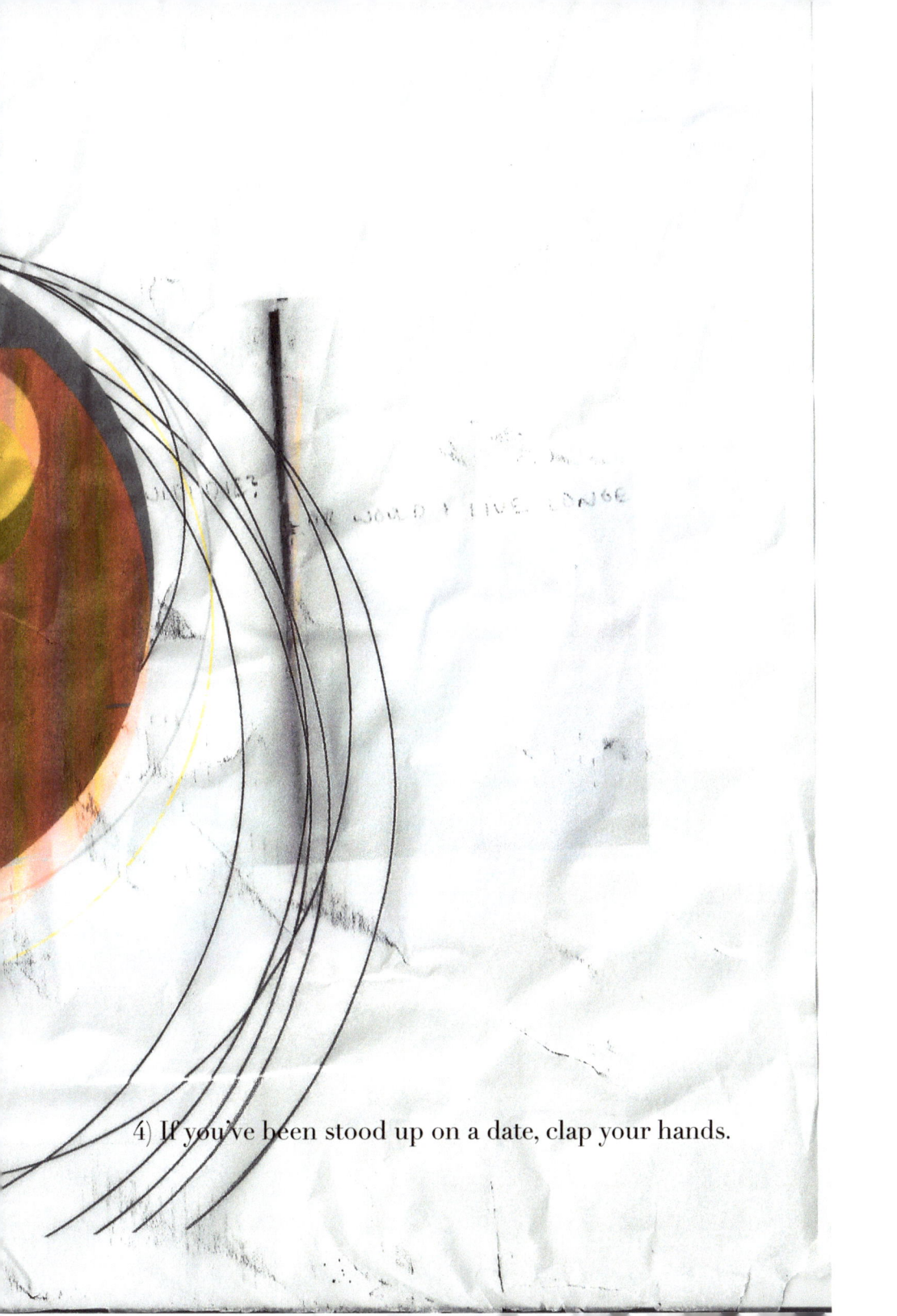

4) If you've been stood up on a date, clap your hands.

5) If you know why a raven is like a writing desk, clap your hands.

6) If you like the smell of autmn in the mountains, clap your hands.

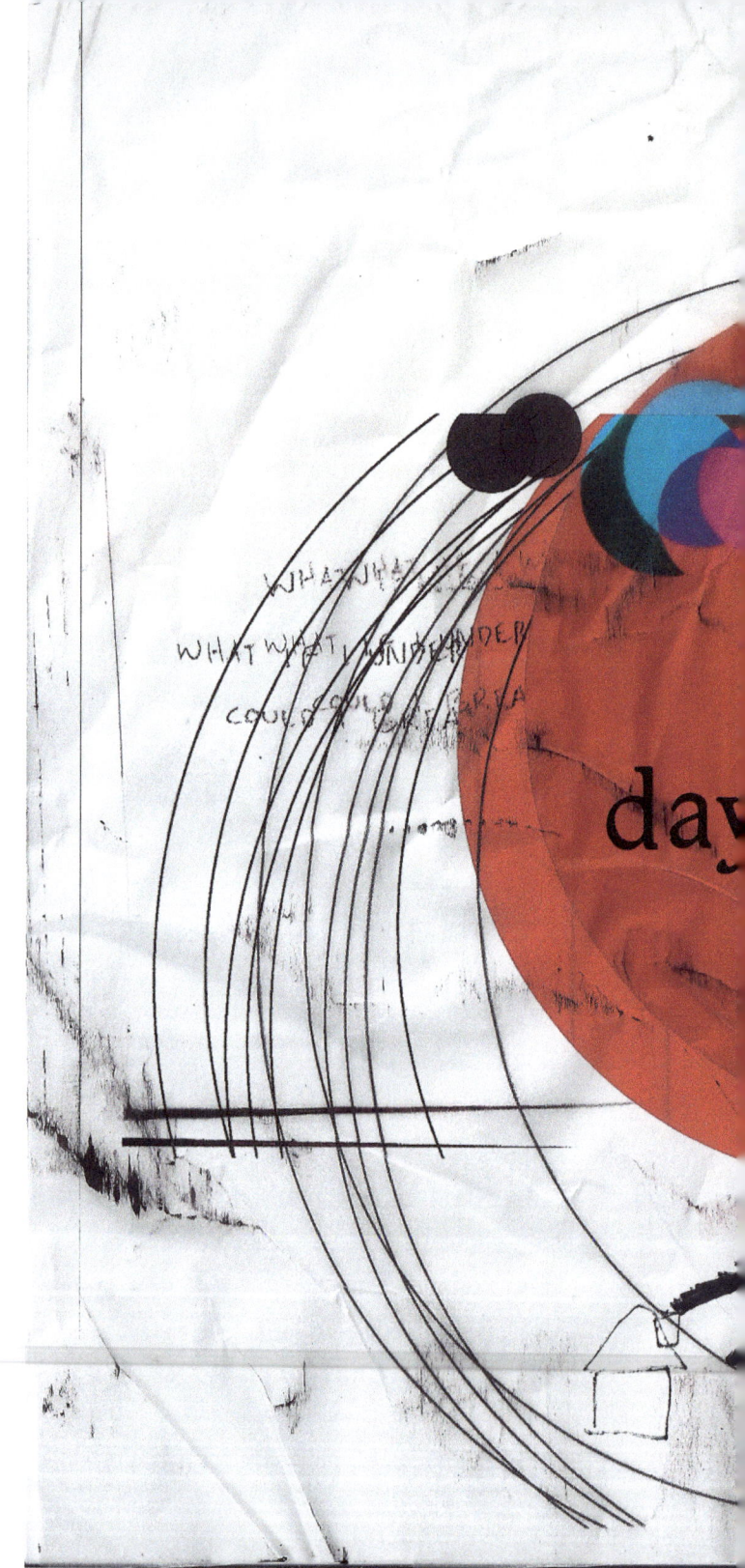

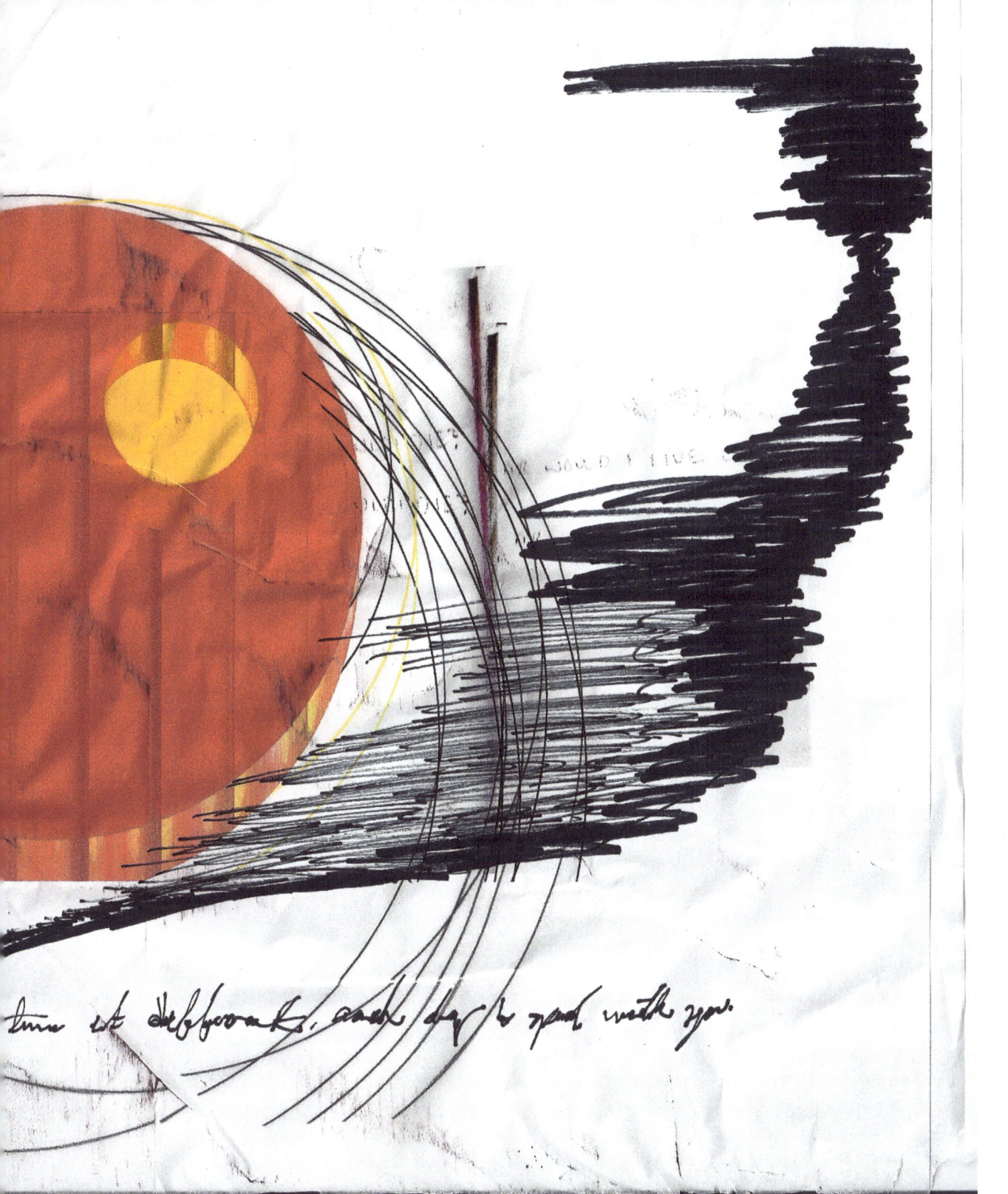

7) If you cry on a regular basis, clap your hands.

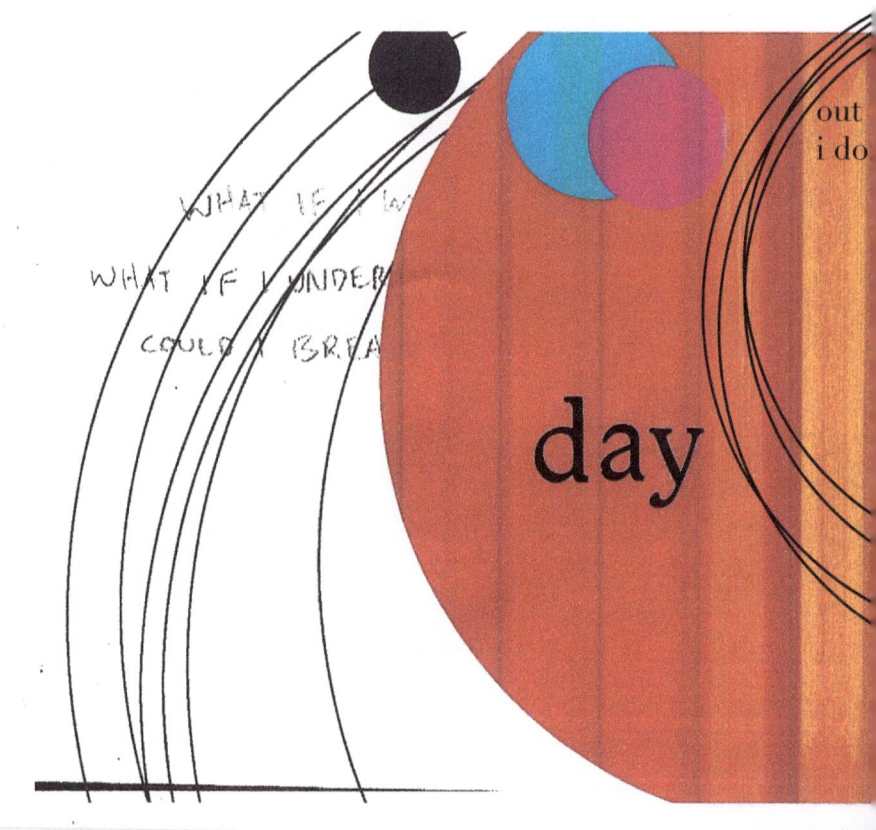

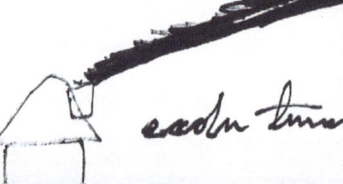

8) If you know why you're in love, clap your hands.

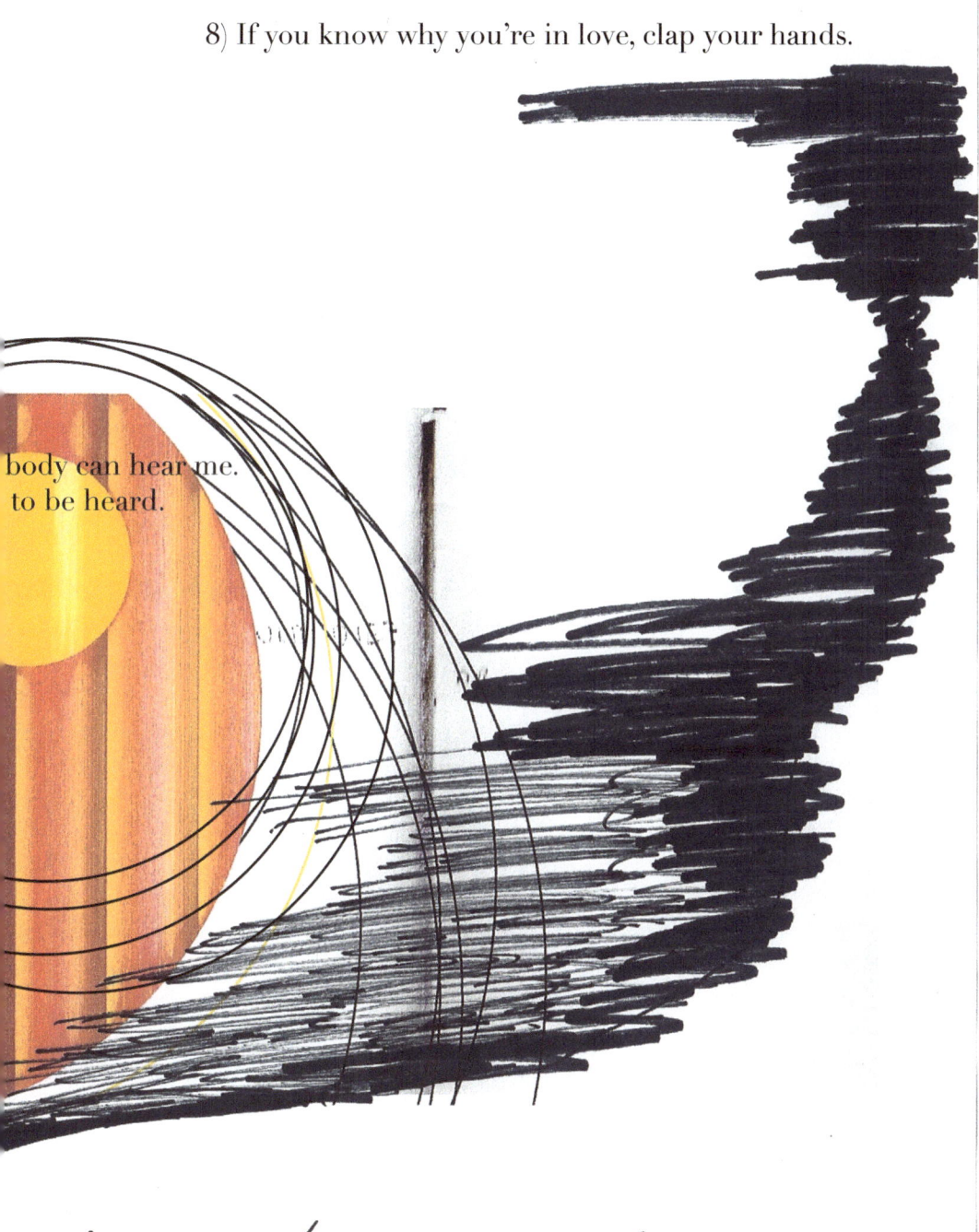

body can hear me.
to be heard.

"did you hear that?"